First World War
and Army of Occupation
War Diary
France, Belgium and Germany

38 DIVISION
115 Infantry Brigade
Royal Welsh Fusiliers
2nd Battalion
1 February 1918 - 30 April 1919

WO95/2561/1

The Naval & Military Press Ltd
www.nmarchive.com
Published in association with The National Archives

Published by

The Naval & Military Press Ltd

Unit 10 Ridgewood Industrial Park,

Uckfield, East Sussex,

TN22 5QE England

Tel: +44 (0) 1825 749494

www.naval-military-press.com

www.nmarchive.com

This diary has been reprinted in facsimile from the original. Any imperfections are inevitably reproduced and the quality may fall short of modern type and cartographic standards.

© **Crown Copyright**
Images reproduced by permission of The National Archives, London, England, 2015.

Contents

Document type	Place/Title	Date From	Date To
Heading	WO95/2561/1 2 Battalion Royal Welsh Fusiliers		
Heading	38th Division 115th Infy Bde 2nd Bn Roy. Welch Fus. Feb 1918-Apr 1919 From 33 Div 19 Bde		
War Diary	Longueness	01/02/1918	04/02/1918
War Diary	Renescure	05/02/1918	05/02/1918
War Diary	Thiennes.	06/02/1918	06/02/1918
War Diary	Robermetz.	07/02/1918	18/02/1918
War Diary	Rolanderie	19/02/1918	21/02/1918
War Diary	Wezmacquart	22/02/1918	28/02/1918
War Diary	Trenches.	01/03/1918	01/03/1918
War Diary	Rolanderie	02/03/1918	09/03/1918
War Diary	Trenches.	10/03/1918	17/03/1918
War Diary	Rolanderie	18/03/1918	25/03/1918
War Diary	Trenches.	26/03/1918	29/03/1918
War Diary	Le Sart	30/03/1918	31/03/1918
Miscellaneous	During the Month the following have been Demobilised Total Demobilised from the Battalion Up to 30/4/19	30/04/1919	30/04/1919
Heading	115th Inf. Bde. 38th Div. War Diary 2nd Battn. The Royal Welch Fusiliers. April. 1918		
War Diary	Le Sart.	01/04/1918	01/04/1918
War Diary	Villers Bocage	02/04/1918	02/04/1918
War Diary	Hedauville	03/04/1918	07/04/1918
War Diary	Herissart	07/04/1918	11/04/1918
War Diary	Millencourt	12/04/1918	18/04/1918
War Diary	Bouzincourt	19/04/1918	26/04/1918
War Diary	Henencourt	27/04/1918	27/04/1918
War Diary	Senlis	28/04/1918	02/05/1918
War Diary	Trenches.	03/05/1918	08/05/1918
War Diary	Senlis.	09/05/1918	14/05/1918
War Diary	Trenches.	15/05/1918	20/05/1918
War Diary	Harponville	21/05/1918	21/05/1918
War Diary	Herissart	22/05/1918	03/06/1918
War Diary	Acheuex Wood	04/06/1918	04/06/1918
War Diary	Mesnil Sector	05/06/1918	10/06/1918
War Diary	Forceville	10/06/1918	22/06/1918
War Diary	Englebelmer	22/06/1918	30/06/1918
War Diary	Forceville	01/07/1918	13/07/1918
War Diary	Support	14/07/1918	18/07/1918
War Diary	Herissart	19/07/1918	30/07/1918
War Diary	Forceville	31/07/1918	05/08/1918
War Diary	Bouzincourt	06/08/1918	11/08/1918
War Diary	Senlis	12/08/1918	15/08/1918
War Diary	Martinsart	16/08/1918	23/08/1918
War Diary	River Ancre	24/08/1918	24/08/1918
War Diary	Contalmaison	25/08/1918	25/08/1918
War Diary	Longueval	26/08/1918	26/08/1918
War Diary	High Wood	27/08/1918	27/08/1918
War Diary	Les Bouefs	28/08/1918	01/09/1918
War Diary	Sailly Saillisel	02/09/1918	02/09/1918
War Diary	Les. Mesnil	03/09/1918	05/09/1918

War Diary	S. of Les Bouefs	06/09/1918	09/09/1918
War Diary	E. of Lechelle	10/09/1918	11/09/1918
War Diary	Gouzeaucourt	12/09/1918	16/09/1918
War Diary	N. of Equancourt	17/09/1918	17/09/1918
War Diary	Fins Ridge	18/09/1918	18/09/1918
War Diary	Dessart Wood	19/09/1918	19/09/1918
War Diary	N. of Beaulencourt	21/09/1918	27/09/1918
War Diary	Sorel Le Grand	28/09/1918	03/10/1918
War Diary	Lempire	04/10/1918	04/10/1918
War Diary	E. of Bony	05/10/1918	05/10/1918
War Diary	Le Catelet	06/10/1918	06/10/1918
War Diary	W. of Pienne	07/10/1918	07/10/1918
War Diary	Villers Outreaux	08/10/1918	09/10/1918
War Diary	Bertry	10/10/1918	11/10/1918
War Diary	Troisville	12/10/1918	13/10/1918
War Diary	Selle River	14/10/1918	18/10/1918
War Diary	Troisville	19/10/1918	21/10/1918
War Diary	River Selle	22/10/1918	22/10/1918
War Diary	Troisville	23/10/1918	23/10/1918
War Diary	Croix	24/10/1918	24/10/1918
War Diary	Forest Englefontaine	25/10/1918	26/10/1918
War Diary	Brasserie	27/10/1918	29/10/1918
War Diary	Croix	30/10/1918	01/11/1918
War Diary	Engle Fontaine	02/11/1918	05/11/1918
War Diary	Foret-De-Mormal	06/11/1918	06/11/1918
War Diary	Berlaimont	07/11/1918	07/11/1918
War Diary	Aulnoye	08/11/1918	29/12/1918
War Diary	Hecq	30/12/1918	30/12/1918
War Diary	Inchy	31/12/1918	31/12/1918
War Diary	Blangy Tronville	01/01/1919	30/04/1919

WO95/2561/1

War Diary 2 Battalion Royal Welch Fusiliers

38TH DIVISION
115TH INFY BDE

2ND BN ROY. WELCH FUS.

FEB 1918-APR 1919

FROM 33 DIV
19 BDE

Army Form C. 2118.

WAR DIARY 2nd Battalion, Royal Welch Fusiliers.
or
INTELLIGENCE SUMMARY.
(Erase heading not required.)

Instructions regarding War Diaries and Intelligence Summaries are contained in F. S. Regs., Part II. and the Staff Manual respectively. Title pages will be prepared in manuscript.

Place	Date	Hour	Summary of Events and Information	Remarks and references to Appendices
LONGUENESSE	1/2/18		Billeted in LONGUENESSE. Specialist Classes and training near billets.	
" do "	2/2/18		Training. 2nd Lieut. R.Nield-Siddall rejoined from hospital.	
" do "	3/2/18		Church parade at No.1 Billet LONGUENESSE.	
" do "	4/2/18		The Battalion moved to RENESCURE on way to join 38th(Welch) Division Address by Major-General R.J.Pinney C.B. and Brigadier General O.R.G.Wayne D.S.O. Pipers of the CAMERONIANS and 5th SCOTTISH RIFLES played the Battalion out of LONGUENESSE.	
RENESCURE	5/2/18		The Battalion moved to THIENNES. Billets good.	
THIENNES.	6/2/18		The Battalion moved to ROBERMETZ. Massed bands and drums of the 115th Infantry Brigade played the Battalion into billets and through MERVILLE. Lieut. G.E.B.Barkworth rejoined from hospital.	
ROBERMETZ.	7/2/18		Billets in ROBERMETZ very good. Whole battalion bathed.	
" do "	8/2/18		Working Parties under 124 Field Coy.R.E., construction of new Corps line. (100 Diggers)	
" do "	9/2/18		Lieut-General Sir J.B.Du CANE C.B., inspected the Battalion at 11-0 a.m. in drill order.	
" do "	10/2/18		Sgt G.W.Worsley "B" Coy awarded the Belgium Croix de Guerre. The following officers joined the Battalion from 19th R.W.F. Lieut. E.J.PRUDHOE posted to "A" Coy.	
			2nd Lieut. O.CRABTREE " "D" "	
			" " J.DIGGLE " "B" "	
			" " A.L.Jones " "B" "	
			" " D.A.AINGE " "C" "	
" do "	10/2/18		Continued working parties.	
" do "	11/2/18		Church parade at Concert Hall, MERVILLE.	
" do "	12/2/18		Continued Working party. Adjutant's Parade at 9-30 a.m.	
			Continued Working party. 2nd Lieut. J.BUTLER posted to "D" Coy and 2nd Lieut. R.WYNNE posted to "B" Coy., joined the Battalion from the Base.	
" do "	13/2/18		Battalion moved to HOLLEBECQUE CAMP in STEENWERCK area and relieved the 1/5th Loyal North Lancs Regt. Very wet.	
" do "	14/2/18		Battalion cleaned up and booked deficiencies.	
" do "	15/2/18		Battalion trained at HOLLEBECQUE CAMP and fired on the range. Office re reconnoitred L'ARMEE and FLEURIE Switches in rear of the WEZ MACQUART Section of the line.	
" do "	16/2/18		Continued training.	
" do "	17/2/18		Church parade in open at HOLLEBECQUE CAMP.	
" do "	18/2/18		The Battalion moved to ROLANDERIE FARM AREA. 3 Companies in ROLANDERIE FARM. 1 Company in houses in L'ARMEE and Battalion Headquarters in ARTILLERY FARM. Men crowded but comfortable.	
ROLANDERIE	19/2/18		O.C.Companies reconnoitred the front line. Companies continued training near billets.	

Army Form C. 2118.

WAR DIARY
2nd Battalion, Royal Welch Fusiliers.
INTELLIGENCE SUMMARY.

– (2) –

(Erase heading not required.)

Instructions regarding War Diaries and Intelligence Summaries are contained in F. S. Regs., Part II. and the Staff Manual respectively. Title pages will be prepared in manuscript.

Place	Date	Hour	Summary of Events and Information	Remarks and references to Appendices
ROLANDERIE	20/2/18		1 Company working for Divisional Signal Officer, reporting at farm at H.5.c.20.25. (Sheet 36A) at 9-0 a.m. Full day's work.	
– do –	21/2/18		1 Company as above, ½ day's work. Battalion relieved 17th R.W.F. in centre and left sector of the WEZ MACQUART Sector "C" and "D" Coys in line ("A" on the right) "A" and "B" Coys in Sub sidiary Line ("B" on right) Relief complete at 9-0 p.m.	
WEZMACQUART	22/2/18		Front line held by posts.	
– do –	23/2/18		Front line trenches. Enemy shelled, left Company.	
– do –	24/2/18		Front line. Quiet 2nd Lieut. H.D.Jones joined from the 19th R.W.F.,	
– do –	25/2/18		Fine and mild.	
– do –	26/2/18		"A" Coy relieved "D" Coy in left sub-sector and "B" Coy relieved "C" Coy in right sub-sector. Trenches.	
– do –	27/2/18		Trenches.	
– do –	28/2/18		Trenches.	

WBarnett

Lieutenant- Colonel.,
Commanding, 2nd Battalion, Royal Welch Fusiliers.

115/38

Army Form C. 2118.

WAR DIARY 2nd Battalion, ROYAL WELCH FUSILIERS
INTELLIGENCE SUMMARY

(Erase heading not required.)

Vol 44

Place	Date	Hour	Summary of Events and Information	Remarks and references to Appendices
TRENCHES.	1st March.18.		St. DAVID'S DAY. Battalion relieved by 17th R.W.F. and marched to ROLANDERIE FARM., Hd Qrs at ARTILLERY FARM. Dinner:- Guests - Brig-General G.Gwyn-Thomas and Staff.	
ROLANDERIE	2nd	"	Rest and cleaning up.	
- do -	3rd	"	3 Companies working party on L'ARMEE SWITCH. 1 Coy working for Divisional Signal Officer.	
- do -	4th	"	Mess Meeting.	
- do -	5th	"	Continued working parties.	
- do -	6th	"	Continued working parties.	
- do -	7th	"	Continued working parties.	
- do -	8th	"	Continued working parties.	
- do -	9th	"	Continued working parties. Battalion relieved 17th R.W.F. in centre and Left Sectors of the WE Z MACQUART Sector. "A" Coy relieved "A" Coy 17/R.W.F. "B" Coy relieved "B" Coy, "D" Coy relieved "D" Coy. Before relief Headquarters at ARTILLERY FARM was shelled, which delayed relief. No casualties.	
TRENCHES.	10th	"	Front line scattered shelling.	
- do -	11th	"	Back areas very heavily shelled. Captain Yates had great difficulty in delivering rations.	
- do -	12th	"	Quiet.	
- do -	13th	"	Early morning a large enemy Raiding Party, about 300, attempted to raid our t post, about 20 succeded in getting through our Artillery barrage and attacked EVEL YN POST held by "D" Coy who repulsed them, inflicting losses and captured one prisoner.	
- do -	14th	"	C.S.M. V.W.WARD D.C.M. appointed 2nd Lieutenant and posted to this Battalion.	
- do -	15th	"	2nd Lieutenant F.M. Hughes attached to Divisional Snipers Company.2nd Lieut. D.A.L.AINGE becomes Battalion Intelligence Officer.	
- do -	16th	"	Enemy shelled Subsidiary Line, principally "C" Coy, with gas shells. 1 gas casualty. "C" Coys Headquarters blown in with direct hit.	
- do -	17th	"	Lieut. F.F.ANNEAR went to Hospital with Shell Shock. Relieved in front line by 17th R.W.F. Enemy shelling back areas, which slightly delayed relief. Battalion and B.H.Q. at LA ROLANDERIE FARM. Slight shelling of the back area.	
ROLANDERIE	18th	"	Captain W.W.KIRKBY rejoined the Battalion from U.K. and is posted to "B" Coy.	
- do -	19th	"	Battalion working party on L'ARMEE SWITCH.	
- do -	20th	"	- do -	
- do -	21st	"	Early morning , whole area gas shelled. Working Party on L'ARMEE SWITCH worked for 3 hours in respirators and had 2 killed and 1 wounded. Worked posponed and resumed at 6-0 p.m. again	

Army Form C. 2118.

WAR DIARY
or
INTELLIGENCE SUMMARY.
(Erase heading not required.)

(2)

Instructions regarding War Diaries and Intelligence Summaries are contained in F. S. Regs., Part II. and the Staff Manual respectively. Title pages will be prepared in manuscript.

Place	Date	Hour	Summary of Events and Information	Remarks and references to Appendices
ROLANDERIE	21st March.		(continued) obliged to cease work on account of shelling. 122 men from "A" and "B" Coys and one platoon each from "C" and "D" Coys kept off working party to practice Raid.	
- do -	22nd	"	Working Party, Raid practice.	
- do -	23rd	"	- do -	
- do -	24th	"	Company Commanders reconnoitred WEZ MACQUART Sector.Divine Services, O of E 9-30 a.m. and Nonconformists 11-0 a.m. in Signallers billets, LA ROLANDERIE.	
- do -	25th	"	Battalion relieved 17th R.W.F. in WEZ MACQUART Sector. "A" Coy LEFT, "B" Coy LEFT CENTRE, "C" Coy RIGHT CENTRE, "D" Coy RIGHT. Very quiet.	
TRENCHES.	26th	"	Altered our dispositions in the line. 3 Coys in front and 1 Coy at FLEURIE SWITCH.	
- do -	27th	"	Quiet day. Shelling at night.	
- do -	28th	"	Quiet day. 1 platoon of "A" Coy LEFT, raided enemy's front line which was found to be unoccupied. Our losses 3 wounded.	
- do -	29th	"	Relieved by 1/5 L.N.Lancs Regt. 170th Brigade, marched to SAILLY. Last Coy arriving about 5-30 a.m.	
LE-SART.	30th	"	Battalion marched to LE SART. Comfortable billets, though rather scattered.	
- do -	31st	"	Battalion at rest in LE SART. Easter Sunday. Voluntary C of E and Nonconformists Services.	

R. Ditheremont Major for
Lieutenant-Colonel,
Commanding, 2nd Battalion, Royal Welch Fusiliers.

Army Form C. 2118.

WAR DIARY
or
INTELLIGENCE SUMMARY.
(Erase heading not required.)

Instructions regarding War Diaries and Intelligence Summaries are contained in F. S. Regs. Part II. and the Staff Manual respectively. Title pages will be prepared in manuscript.

Place	Date	Hour	Summary of Events and Information	Remarks and references to Appendices
			During the Month the following have been demobilised :-	
			Total demobilised from the Battalion up to 30/4/19 :-	
			Officers. O. Ranks. Miners. TOTAL.	
			3 14	
			8 206	
			422	
			8 628.	
			To 26th Bn. Royal Welsh Fusiliers up to 30/4/19 :-	
			8 68.	

Shaw Capt a/Adjt

for CAPTAIN.

COMMANDING 2nd. ROYAL WELSH FUSILIERS.

115th Inf.Bde.
38th Div.

WAR DIARY

2nd BATTN. THE ROYAL WELCH FUSILIERS.

A P R I L

1 9 1 8

Army Form C. 2118.

WAR DIARY
or
INTELLIGENCE SUMMARY.

2nd Battalion, ROYAL WELCH FUSILIERS.

(Erase heading not required.)

Instructions regarding War Diaries and Intelligence Summaries are contained in F. S. Regs., Part II. and the Staff Manual respectively. Title pages will be prepared in manuscript.

JA 45

HHN
2 sheets

Place	Date	Hour	Summary of Events and Information	Remarks and references to Appendices
LE SART. VILLERS-BOCAGE.	1st April, 19.		Moved by rail, entraining at CALONNE, to DOULENS.	
VILLERS-BOCAGE	2nd		Moved to HEDAUVILLE.	
HEDAUVILLE.	3rd		Billets in HEDAUVILLE. Marched from DOULENS to VILLERS-BOCAGE.	
- do -	4th	"	Billets in HEDAUVILLE fair. Working party of 1/5 working on trenches near ENGLEBELMER. Very wet.	
- do -	5th	"	Range allotted to Companies. Rain. Working Party of 350 on the trenches near ENGLEBELMER.	
- do -	6th	"	Range allotted to Companies.	
- do -	7th	"		
HERRISSART.	8th	"	Moved by road to HERRISART. Lieut.F.F.Arnear struck off Battalion strength, evacuated to England, sick. Billets poor.	
- do -	9th	"	Billets in HERRISART. Rain.	
- do -	10th	"	"	
- do -	11th	"	Relieved 13th Battalion of the Welsh Regt as Right Battalion of Brigade in reserve near MILENCOURT. Battle Surplus to CONTAY, about 15 Officers and 144 Other ranks. Lieut-Colonel W.B. Garnett D.S.O. remained with the Battle Surplus. Major G. E. R. de Miremont in command of the Battalion in the line.	
MILENCOURT.	12th	"	Lieut. Wm MACDONALD, 2nd Lieut. S.S. JACK and 2nd Lieut. JasMARY AND, joined the Battalion from the Battalion from the 1st Entrenching Battalion, formerly 15/R. W.F.	
- do -	13th	"	50% of the Battle Surplus moved to V Corps Reinforcement Camp, ORAMONT. Battalion in bivouacs near MILENCOURT.	
- do -	14th	"	12 men withdrawn from the line to Battle Surplus for Lewis Gun instruction. Battalion detailed for work on Corps Line from 9-0 p.m. to 1-0 a.m. Very dark night.	
- do -	15th	"	All Battle surplus bathed at CONTAY. Battalion in bivouacs near MILENCOURT working on Corps Line near SENLIS from 10-0 p.m. to 2-0 a.m.	
- do -	16th	"	Battalion in bivouacs near MILENCOURT. No working party.	
- do -	17th	"	Battalion in bivouacs near MILENCOURT. Working party cancelled.	
- do -	18th	"	Lewis Gun class fired on the range (30 yards). Battalion relieved the 15/R.W.F. in the Right Sub-Section of the Left Brigade Sub-Sector. Right Coy "D". Centre Coy "B". Left Coy "B" Support Coy "A".	
BOUZINCOURT.	19th	"	Battalion relieved 15/R.W.F. in Right sector of Brigade near BOUZINCOURT. "D" Coy on Right "C" Coy on left. "B" Coy support "A" Coy in reserve. Quiet in night. H.Q. very uncomfortable. Men in disconnected trenches "A" Coy. dug in, in bank. Lewis Gun fired on long range in the morning (and 50 yds in left bracon. Battalion in trenches. Quiet except for a little hostile shelling, and machine gun fire. Very cold with sharp frost.	

Army Form C. 2118.

WAR DIARY
or
INTELLIGENCE SUMMARY.
(Erase heading not required.)

- (2) -

Instructions regarding War Diaries and Intelligence Summaries are contained in F. S. Regs., Part II. and the Staff Manual respectively. Title pages will be prepared in manuscript.

Place	Date	Hour	Summary of Events and Information	Remarks and references to Appendices
BOUZINCOURT.	20th April, 15		Lewis Gun fired on range in afternoon. Battalion in trenches. Very cold. Slight shelling throughout night, and machine-gun fire at night.	As
- do -	21st "		12 men returned to the line as Lewis Gunners from Battle Surplus, 12 more sent down for training. Sunday. Fine day. Church parade O of E :- 9-15 a.m. Nonconfor 1st :- 10-30 a.m. Battalion in trenches. Usual machine gun and artillery fire. Bright moonlight night. "G" Oey Left front Oey, relieved by 13/R.W.F. "C" Oey fell back in line with "B" Oey. (Support) "C" Oey ordered to occupy its old position, when 13/R.W.F. attacked.	As As
- do -	22nd "		Battalion in trenches. Minor operations carried out by 115th Inf. Bde. ordered to send "A" Oey (Reserve) in support to 16/R.W.F. Attack partly successful. 13 men ordered to reinforce with 3 Platoons of "G" Oey. Enemy artillery quiet. About 40 prisoners including an officer passed Battalion H.Q. Our casualties slight.	As As
- do -	23rd "		About 2-0 a.m. ordered to reinforce 13/R.W.F. with 3 more plat oons sent Nos.5, 6, & 8 of "B" Oey. 13th Wel Bn, (Battalion on Right) lent Battalion 1 Oey of 3 pla toons to make up deficiency through reinforcing 13/R.W.F. Enemy lively.	As As
- do -	24th "		Battalion expected to be relieved but relief cancelled.	As
- do -	25th "		Battalion relieved by 10/S.W.B. and moved to sunken road near BOUZINCOURT in support.	As
- do -	26th "		Battalion relieved by 10/S.W.B. and moved to Sunken road near HENENCOURT Wood.	As
HENENCOURT.	27th "		In evening Battalion moved to sunken roads South of SENLIS. H.Q. orderly Room forced to move	As
SENLIS.	28th "		Battalion near SENLIS. Enemy active. Battalion supplied working party of 3 Oeys for work on Corps and old French Line S of BOUZINCOURT and near SENLIS Mill.	As
- do -	29th "		Battalion still near SENLIS. Supplied working party of 3 Oeys on Corps Line S of BOUZINCOURT.	As
- do -	30th "		Battalion still near SENLIS Supplied working party of 3 Oeys o n Corps Line S of BOUZINCOURT. Battle Surplus under Lieut-Colonel W.B. Garnett D.S.O. went to DOMQUEUR LE PLOUY.	As

signature

for O.C. 2nd Battalion, Royal Welch Fusiliers.

2nd Lieutenant,

Army Form C. 2118.

WAR DIARY
or
INTELLIGENCE SUMMARY.
(Erase heading not required.)

2nd Battalion, ROYAL WELCH FUSILIERS.

Vol 46

Place	Date	Hour	Summary of Events and Information	Remarks and references to Appendices
SENLIS.	1st May, 18.		Battalion in sunken road near SENLIS. Supplied working parties of 3 Companies for work on Corps line South of BOUZINCOURT.	
- do -	2nd " "		Battalion in sunken road near SENLIS. Relieved 1/R.W.F. in right sub sector of Brigade. "A" Coy Right Front. "B" Coy Left Front. "C" Coy in support. "D" Coy in reserve.	
TRENCHES.	3rd " "		Battalion in trenches. Quiet.	
- do -	4th " "		- do -	
- do -	5th " "		- do -	
- do -	6th " "		"B" Coy attempted a raid on enemy post, failed owing to weath-r conditions and alertness of enemy. About 10-50 p.m Lieutenant J.T.S. EVANS and 1 other rank were captured whilst out on patrol. Both reported wounded.	
- do -	7th " "		Battalion in trenches. Very quiet night.	
- do -	8th " "		Battalion relieved by 17/R.W.F. Relief soon and heavily shelled. No casualties. To sunken road South of SENLIS.	
SENLIS.	9th " "		Battalion in sunken road south of SENLIS. Enemy attacked the Battalion on right of 17/R.W.F. (23rd London Regt) and occupied the front line. Major G.E.R. de Miremont made A/Lieut-Colonel whilst commanding the battalion.	
SENLIS.	10th " "		Battalion in sunken road South of SENLIS. Supplied Companies working in old French and Corps Lines. Coy wiring and 3 Coys digging. Enemy driven out of front line by 23rd London Regt Line intact.	
SENLIS.	11th " "		Supplied 4 Coys for work as per 10th. Military Medal awarded to No. 11424 Sgt Turrell Wm, and 524 123 L/Cpl Jeremiah JONES.	
SENLIS.	12th " "		- do -	
- d -	13th " "		Working parties as per 10th.	
- do -	14th " "		Battalion relieved 10/S.W.B. in the left Sector of Brigade East of BOUZINCOURT. Quiet relief. "C" Coy - Right Front. "D" Coy - Left Front. "A" Coy in support. "B" Coy in reserve.	
TRENCHES.	15th " "		H.Qrs lightly shelled during the day.	
- do -	16th " "		Quiet day. H.Q. moved from cellar in BOUZINCOURT to sunken road S of BOUZINCOURT.	
- do -	17th " "		Quiet day.	
- do -	18th " "		Enemy lightly shelled area near battalion H.Q. At 11-0 a.m. an enemy heavily shelled the left Company and support in retaliation of raid carried out by left battalion 1st/R.W.F. Very hot weather.	

Army Form C. 2118.

WAR DIARY
or
INTELLIGENCE SUMMARY.

2nd Battalion, Royal Welch Fusiliers.

(Erase heading not required.)

- (2) -

Place	Date	Hour	Summary of Events and Information	Remarks and references to Appendices
TRENCHES.	19th May.		At 5-0 a.m. enemy heavily shelled whole battalion area. 3 killed and 8 wounded. Support and reserve areas shelled at intervals during morning. Very hot weather.	
- do -	20th		Battalion relieved by 8th North Staffs Regt. Relief shelled and heavily gassed. Relief complete 2-20 a.m.	
HARPONVILLE	21st		Battalion marched to position near HARPONVILLE for breakfast. Marched to Camp S.E. of HERISSART. Very hot.	
HERISSART.	22nd		Battalion in camp near HERISSART. Many cases of gas poisoning. Battalion cleaned up.	
- do -	23rd		Captain J.C. DUNN, D.S.O., M.C., D.C.M., R.A.M.C., evacuated gassed. Whole battalion bathed and clothes put through ODEN Disinctor.	
- do -	24th		Commenced training and rifle competitions.	
- do -	25th		Continued training.	
- do -	2'th		Continued training.	
- do -	27th		Church Parade.	
- do -	28th		Battalion and transport inspected by Corps General, Major General LUHUTE, V Corps. Battalion and transport especially congratulated on its clean turn-out.	
- do -	29th		Tactical scheme in co-operation with tanks.	
- do -	30th		Continued training. Rifle and sports competitions. TOUHE died.	
- do -	31st		Half-battalion bathed. Continued training etc. Remainder of battalion bathed. Brigade tactical scheme for officers, runners and signallers.etc.	

R. [signature]
Capt. Adjt.

for Lieutenant-Colonel,
Commanding, 2nd Battalion, Royal Welch Fusiliers.",

WAR DIARY 2nd Battalion Royal Welch Fusiliers

Army Form C. 2118.

or

INTELLIGENCE SUMMARY.

(Erase heading not required.)

Instructions regarding War Diaries and Intelligence Summaries are contained in F. S. Regs., Part II. and the Staff Manual respectively. Title pages will be prepared in manuscript.

Place	Date	Hour	Summary of Events and Information	Remarks and references to Appendices
HERISSART	June 1st 1918		Battalion in camp. Voluntary Church Service.	P.W.
— Do —	" 2nd "		— Do —	P.W.
— Do —	" 3rd "		Battalion marched to camp in ACHEUX WOOD. Battle emphet to HIERMONT, King's Birthday Honour LONDON GAZETTE dated 2nd June: — Military Cross: — Capt H. Yates, No 55788 R.S.M. Brecknow AM. DCM., - 90146 R.A.M.S. Hughes J., 8233 Sgt Meredith J. mentioned in Despatches: 1st Lt Col W.B. Garrett D.S.O., Capt R. Mostyn M.C., 2nd Lt T.H. Williamson 51456 Y/c Kee Y., 11396 Sgt Johnson.	P.W.
ACHEUX WOOD	June 4th		Battalion relieves Hawke Battalion. 63rd Naval Division on the centre MESNIL SECTOR. Dispositions "A" Coy relieves "A" Coy Right front, "B" Coy relieves "B" Coy. Left front. "C" Coy relieves "C" Coy Right support. "D" Coy relieves "D" Coy. Left support. Quiet relief.	P.W.
MESNIL SECTOR	June 5th		Beautiful weather. Quiet day.	P.W.
"	6th		Change in disposition. Left Half Battalion relieved by 14th R.W.F. 113th Brigade very late relief complete 5-20 A.M. "C" Coy front "D" Coy support "B" B Coy Reserve "D" Coy No 3 Defended Locality, in Lieu O.T. RICKETTS & 2nd Lieut R. WYNNE posted to 115th L.T.M. B.	P.W.
"	7th		Quiet day. Heavy bombardment on our left in the evening. Lt E.T.E. GWALCHMAI evacuated to UK sick, gun abroad off when left 30.5.1918.	P.W.
"	8th		14th Division inches with this Battalion on our left. We co-operated by discharging rockets. Did not do any annoying artillery fire.	P.W.
"	9th		Quiet. Slight Rain.	P.W.

WAR DIARY 2nd Battalion, Royal Welch Fusiliers

INTELLIGENCE SUMMARY

Army Form C. 2118.

(Erase heading not required.)

Place	Date	Hour	Summary of Events and Information	Remarks and references to Appendices
MESNIL SECTOR	April 9th		Enemy artillery slightly more	Ref.
FORCEVILLE	" 10th		Change of disposition, "B" Coy relieved "C" Coy, "A" Coy in the front line, "B" Coy in Reserve. "B" Coy No 3 defended locality.	Ref.
"	11-12th		"C" Coy front line relieved by "A" Coy, 14th R.W.F. "D" Coy front line relieved by 1 Coy, Battalion moved to "PURPLE SYSTEM" (Reserve Battn.)	Ref.
"	12th 13th		Battalion moved into Aird Reserve near FORCEVILLE.	Ref.
"	13th		Battalion practice for counterattack Rase. Training near WEST LEALVILLERS Battn. B. by 1st & D.	Ref.
"	14th		At	Ref.
"	15th		Training for Raid	Ref.
"	16th		do	Ref.
"	17th		do	Ref.
"	18th		do	Ref.
"	19th		do	Ref.
"	20th		Battalion R.U.	Ref.
"	21st		Battalion carried out a raid on enemy line N. of AVELUY WOOD. Trenches from to attack or No Prisoners or material obtained. ZERO 2 A.M. May not right-	Ref.
"	22nd		Battalion cleaning up.	Ref.

WAR DIARY 2nd Battalion Royal Welch Fusiliers
INTELLIGENCE SUMMARY

Army Form C. 2118.

Place	Date	Hour	Summary of Events and Information	Remarks and references to Appendices
ENGLEBELMER	23rd August		Battalion moved to Bivouac EAST of ENGLEBELMER in support & relieved 13th R.W.F.	Plan
"	"		Working parties. Strength 290 OR. Work mainly RE operations on new defences.	Plan
"	24th		1 Officer & 1 O.R. of "B" Coy attached to enemy line W of HAMEL. No enemy were encountered.	Plan
"	25th		Working parties as above.	Plan
"	26th		2 Officers & 30 men of "B" Coy attempted entering our lines in enemy line near HAMEL. Enemy were seen & fired at several enemy outposts. No prisoners & no identifications obtained. No casualties.	Plan
"	27th		Working parties as usual. 2 Officers & 30 men of "B" Coy attempted to procure prisoners & identifications but failed to find enemy. 2 casualties. Working parties as usual.	Plan
"	28th		1 Officer & 30 men of "B" Coy attempted a raid on enemy post near HAMEL. Enemy were in strength & the attempt failed. No casualties.	Plan
"	29th		Battalion relieved 13th Welch Regt. in MESNIL RIGHT SECTOR. "D" Coy right front Coy, "A" Coy Right support Coy, "B" Coy Left support Coy, "C" Coy Left front Coy. (A.P.L. Loop) no incidents to report. Relief complete 10.30 p.m. Relieving Battn one Bn of Welch.	Plan
"	30th		Quiet day.	Plan

R.J. Jones Lt for O.C. 2 Welch Fus

Army Form C. 2118.

WAR DIARY
or
INTELLIGENCE SUMMARY
(Erase heading not required.)

2nd Battalion, Royal Welch Fusiliers.

Instructions regarding War Diaries and Intelligence Summaries are contained in F. S. Regs., Part II. and the Staff Manual respectively. Title pages will be prepared in manuscript.

Place	Date	Hour	Summary of Events and Information	Remarks and references to Appendices
FORCEVILLE	1918 July 1st		Relieved night 1st/2nd by 13/R.W.F. Enemy raided Post in AVELUY WOOD (About 1 officer 20 O.Rs) at 10-0 p.m. Repulsed by "D" Coy. Casualties 6. No one missing. Relief held up on account of Raid. Relief complete at 4.15 a.m. Battalion moved to bivouacs near FORCEVILLE.	Rs
do -	2nd	"	Cleaning up.	Rs
do -	3rd	"	Baths at FORCEVILLE.	Rs
do -	4th	"	Working Parties.	Rs
do -	5th	"	Company training and range practice. 50 O.Rs in FORCEVILLE. 1 Company (100 O.Rs) Cable burying. Brevet Lieutenant-Colonel J.B. Cockburn, from 17/R.W.F. assumed command of the Battalion vice A/Lieut-Colonel G.E.R. de Miremont. Captain (A/Major) G.E.R. de Miremont is appointed 2nd in Command vice A/Major J. Cuthbert M.C. Captain (A/Major) J. Cuthbert M.C. is posted as 2nd in command to 14/R.W.F.	Rs Rs
do -	6th	"	Company Training and preliminary training for Raid.	Rs
do -	7th	"	Company and Battalion practice for Raid on special Training Ground.	Rs
do -	8th	"	- do -	Rs
do -	9th	"	- do -	Rs
do -	10th	"	Final practice. Lecture on Artillery barrage by Lt-Col MACLELLAND D.S.O., R.F.A., Corps Comdr watched final Practice. Shelled on way back to camp. 2 men of "D" Coy wounded. Battalion moved up into INTERMEDIARY SYSTEM in part of ENGLEBELMER and occupied QUACKER ALLEY and front line Intermediary System.	Rs
- do -	11th	"	Companies moved up to assembly trenches at 9-0 p.m. and were in position there by 10-0 p.m. Tapes laid out and all Raiding Companies assembled outside our wire by 10.45 p.m. 11-0 p.m. ZERO when 4 Companies raided HAMEL under Artillery and Machine Gun barrage. 19 prisoners taken and 1 machine gun, over 50 killed and some 20 du gouts blown up. Parties out one hour and withdrew in good order. Very Successful Raid. Casualties :- 2nd Lieut. W.R.Lloyd Killed. Lt Briercliffe, 2nd Lieuts Snedden & Smith Wounded. Wounded (at duty) 2nd Lieut. C.G. Davies. 2.O.Rs. Killed 3. O.Rs. Wnd & Missing. 44.O.Rs Wounded. 3 .O.Rs. Wnd (at duty). 5.O.Rs. Missing. R.Es (attached):- 2 Wounded. Battalion returned to camp at FORCEVILLE.	Rs
- do -	12th	"	Resting. Battalion addressed by the Divisional General- (Major General T.A. CUBITT CMG.DSO.) and complimented on their splendid work.	Rs
- do -	13th	"	Baths at FORCEVILLE. Battalion marched up to SUPPORT occupying INTERMEDIATE SYSTEM. Lieut-Colonel J.B. Cockburn temporarily commanding 115th Inf.Bde. Relieved 13/R.W.F. Good relief. No casualties.	Rs

WAR DIARY

2nd Battalion, Royal Welch Fusiliers.

or

INTELLIGENCE SUMMARY.

Army Form C. 2118.

— (2) —

(Erase heading not required.)

Instructions regarding War Diaries and Intelligence Summaries are contained in F. S. Regs., Part II. and the Staff Manual respectively. Title pages will be prepared in manuscript.

Place	Date 1918.	Hour	Summary of Events and Information	Remarks and references to Appendices
SUPPORT.	14th July.		Quiet day. All Companies on working parties at night.	
- do -	15th "		Quiet day. Officers of 7th Leicester Regt reconnoitred line. Working parties. Establishing -S.A.A.- Reserve in trenches.	
- do -	16th "		Quiet day.	
- do -	17th "		- do -	
- do -	18th "		Battalion relieved as follows :- 2 Companies by 4th Bedfords. 2 Companies by 12th Manchester Regt.	
HERISSART	19th "		Quiet: relief.	
- do -	20th "		Marched to billets in HERISSART. Training. Congratulatory letter received from General BYNG Commanding 3rd Army and Lieut-General SCHUTE V Corps., on success of Raid on 11/7/18.	
- do -	21st "		Training.	
- do -	22nd "		Training. No.70205 L/Cpl J. HILL awarded bar to MILITARY MEDAL. The MILITARY MEDAL was awarded to the following :- 48873 Pte R.Roth well. 27045 L/Sgt W.C.Grey. 21241 Pte S.Metcalfe. 207094 Pte H.M. Humphreys.	
- do -	23rd "		Training. Baths.	
- do -	24th "		Training. The following Officers reported for duty :- Lieut. F. CHICK., 2nd Lieuts H. Turner MM and E.A. Morris MM	
- do -	25th "		Training all day. Very wet.	
- do -	26th "		Battalion inoculated. Very wet.	
- do -	27th "		Training ½ day. Wet.	
- do -	28th "		Church Parade.	
- do -	29th "		Holiday. Brigade Sports Meeting at RUBEMPRE. Battalion moved forward to area near FOREVILLE and ACHEUX. Camp. Very hot march. Regimental Goat died from heat stroke.	
FOREVILLE	31st "		Training. Very hot.	

J.B.Cockburn
Lieutenant-Colonel,
Commanding, 2nd Battalion, Royal Welch Fusiliers.

2/R.W.Fus.
115/38
Army Form C. 2118.
9W 49

WAR DIARY
or
INTELLIGENCE SUMMARY.
(Erase heading not required.) 2nd Bn ROYAL WELCH FUSILIERS

Instructions regarding War Diaries and Intelligence Summaries are contained in F. S. Regs., Part II. and the Staff Manual respectively. Title pages will be prepared in manuscript.

Place	Date	Hour	Summary of Events and Information	Remarks and references to Appendices
FORCEVILLE	1-8-18		Whole Battalion digging BROWN LINE near BEAUSSART	
"	2-8-18		do	
"	3-8-18		do	
"	4-8-18		Training and Bath in the morning.	
"	5-8-18		Tour during Relieved 6th DORSETS in the BOUZINCOURT Sect. "B" & "D" Coy. in Front. "A" Coy Left Support. "D" Coy Right Support. Good Relief	
BOUZINCOURT	6-8-18		38th Divisional Sports	
"	7-8-18		Quiet day. Night Patrols from B & C Coy	
"	8-8-18		Quiet day. Patrol at night examining River ANCRE and running. Beautiful weather. no enemy activity except slight shelling	
"	9-8-18		Stn Coy relief. R Coy relieved "B" Coy. "D" Coy relieved "C" Coy. Patrols as usual	
"	10-8-18		2nd day in front. Army on our right attacked. During our night flank attacked BOUZINCOURT heavily shelled during attack.	
"	11-8-18		A Coy on the Right relieved 20 dark. Battalion relieved by 17/R.W.F. and went into reserve behind SENLIS. Rear ratly. The camp very uncomfortable. Captain P. Mordy M.C. rejoined. Left for U.K. "B" Coy handed Brigade guard.	
SENLIS	12-8-18		Baths for half the Battalion. 2nd Lieut H Evans appointed Adjutant vice Capt Mordy M.C. Battn for remainder. Boy Cleaning up new around camp	
"	13-8-18		Boy Training (morning). L.O. visited Camps Sokert. Battalion relieved 13 and 16 ct NELSH Bhs Divisional Sector MARTINSART-AVELUY WOOD	
"	14-8-18			
"	15-8-18			
MARTINSART	16-8-18		Quiet day. 2 Patrols at night - same ruck.	
"	17-8-18		Working Parties under R.E. found by "A" & "D" Coys 60mm and M.G. Emplacements	
"	18-8-18		Taking Parties as above A and Boy 75 mm and M.G emplacements 1 patrol - River	
"	19-8-18		Working Parties Satr. for day. A/D relieved C & B Coys respectively 1 Patrol (2/Lt Marie) ended river ANCRE and reconnd track. Working Parties A-D and Night Patrols by B & C.	
"	20-8-18		C.O. Coys moved from PURPLE LINE up into Support. Working Parties in could on account of projected move across ANCRE. 2/Lieut. J O Smith and a patrol crossing experimentally attempting crossing near ANCRE	

WAR DIARY
or
INTELLIGENCE SUMMARY.
(Erase heading not required.)

Army Form C. 2118.

- (2) -

Instructions regarding War Diaries and Intelligence Summaries are contained in F.S. Regs., Part II. and the Staff Manual respectively. Title pages will be prepared in manuscript.

Place	Date	Hour	Summary of Events and Information	Remarks and references to Appendices
MARTINSART	21.8.18		No men forward but patrols busy establishing covering at AVELUY	M.
			taken by a which on Railway embankment	
	22.8.18		A Coy pushed across ANCRE and established bridgehead capturing enemy post at	M.
			CRUCIFIX CORNER. Several enemy killed, 10 prisoners and 4 M.G. taken	
			2nd Lieuts D JONES and H Y EVANS found Bath.	
	23.8.18		Adv H Coy crossed East of River and assembled for attack due East on the through	M.
		3.30 am	Bgde. 1.30 am 24th. Very successful attack: over 200 prisoners and 17 M.Gs. taken	
		6 am	Our casualties under 30. 2nd Lieut. BARLOW & 2/Lt JONES wounded	
RIVER ANCRE	24.8.18		Battalion H assembled on East Bank of River & spent the day this	M.
			Bn H+a moved forward at 4.0 pm to Elim. Triangle and held forward with rest	
			of Division. Moved forward southward all night until 4.0 am 25th.	
CONTALMAISON	25.8.18		No opposition met. POZIERES & CONTALMAISON taken. Position established	M.
			N.N. of MAMETZ WOOD. C Coy pushed through BAZENTIN-LE-PETIT Wood and	
			met with violent opposition and forced back to quarries line	
			But C Coy & 2/Lieut. LOLEY wounded. Several casualties to coy. B Coy	
			Battalion attacked to 113 Bde & found enemy in station. The Bde made an	
			attack in BAZENTIN-LE-GRAND - LONGUEVAL. Bn 4 a.m. A.V.C Coy in support	
			R&D Coy right. B Lieut took Bde to Bn. Met opposition on ridge towards	
			BAZENTIN-LE-GRAND especially M.G. fire from ridge about MONTAUBAN. Bn established	
			just East of BAZENTIN-LE-GRAND. Casualties in other Coys heavy.	
			Lt. Col. J B Cockburn wounded in leg. Capt. E J Evans assume command.	
			2/Lieut D L Evans killed (Braeth) whilst in command of what of C Coy	
			A+B Coy approx 115/BH & attached to 10/S.W.B. & 17/R.W.B. respectively	
LONGUEVAL	26.8.18		113 Bde made new LONGUEVAL and GUILLY. 2 Coy, NHQ 2/R.W.F. in Adv.	M.
			but ordered to H from 115 Bde at noon. This done by 12.0 noon	
			Battalion established in trenches S. of HIGH WOOD & subjected to heavy shelling	
HIGH WOOD	27.8.18		Battalion in same position. Reinforcements (Officers) arrived 2/Lt CHATFIELD M.C	M.
			J I E Jones M.C. & V W HUSSEY DCC (for Adjutant Supplies) and 2/Lt LC TAVERTOFT	
			2/Lieut. HOWARD and V.M. SCOTT from U.K. Major J E Le MESURIER joined Bn at	
		10.am. 28th	and assumed command	
			Later E J. Evans	

D. D. & I., London, E.C.
(A8091) Wt. W7:71/M2093 750,000 5/17 Sch. 52 Forms/C2.118/14

Army Form C. 2118.

WAR DIARY
or
INTELLIGENCE SUMMARY.

(Erase heading not required.)

— (3) —

Place	Date	Hour	Summary of Events and Information	Remarks and references to Appendices
LES BOUEFS	28.8.18		115 Bde attacked Eastwards moving on MORVAL and LES BOUEFS. 10/SWB & 17/RWF in front. 2/RWF in support & finding left flank jonc 3.45 a.m. Were found much enfil. barrage. No opposition met with. Zero objective - starting S.W. of LES BOUEFS. Some 20 prisoners taken by Brigade. Much opposition met from LES BOUEFS and MORVAL RIDGE. 10/SWB pushed in support of 10/SWB & 17/RWB. LES BOUEFS are held up their lying 2/RWF employed in support of 10/SWB & 17/RWB.	B
"	29.8.18		Battalion in same position & stood to attack on B.E.B. Several casualties 2/Lt NARD and SCOTT wounded. Major R/A Adamson injured. Tony took command of "B" Coy. Br. M.R. established in Old German Hospital near Railway. Enfield to much shelling.	M
"	30.8.18		Battalion still in front of LES BOUEFS, subject to heavy shelling. Bn also moved to Flannelled N. of hospital on account of enemy shelling	M
"	31.8.18		Battalion established as on 30th August. No change in situation	M

[signature]

2nd Lieutenant
Adjutant for O.C. 2nd Bn RWF...

WAR DIARY
INTELLIGENCE SUMMARY
(Erase heading not required)

Army Form C. 2118.

Place	Date	Hour	Summary of Events and Information	Remarks and references to Appendices
LES BOEUFS.	1.9.18		3rd Division attacked MORVAL & SAILLY-SAILLISEL. 114th Bde. attacked MORVAL, 2nd hour of assault. 115th Inf. Bde attacked SAILLY-SAILLISEL. 2nd hour of assault. 1st by Bde. in support. 2nd R.W.F. were Left assaulting Battalion of the 115th Inf. Bde. with 17th R.W.F. as right assaulting Battalion. 10th D.W.R. in support. The 2nd R.W.F. was formed up at 1.30 am for attack with 'C' & 'D' Front Coys on BAPAUME road just E of LES. BOEUFS. and 'B' 'A' Support Coys in rear on the LES. BOEUFS - LE TRANSLOY Road, with their right resting on LES BOEUFS Church. From 4.45am, when the 114th of Bde attacked and captured MORVAL, till 5.45am, when the 115th Bde advanced, the battalion was lying under an allied Enemy barrage. At 6.30 am the first objective, a road crossing the MORVAL - ROCQUIGNY road, on a ridge was reached & the leading Coys were pushing down into the valley which had to be crossed before reaching the slopes leading up to SAILLY SAILLISEL. The Enemy, who were established in trenches in the valley & the slopes leading to it opened heavy MG and rifle fire, with T.M. & rifle grenade fire. In the meantime LE TRANSLOY which was reported to be in the hands of the 17th Division was found to be in Enemy hands and the Battalion of the 17th Div. which was to operate on our left was held up from the commencement of the attack, with the result that the left flank of the 2/R.W.F. was completely in the air. The Enemy commenced to attack the left flank of the 2/R.W.F. at 7.0 am. This attack developed first against the 2 front Coys, then against the 2 support Coys and eventually from LE TRANSLOY itself against advanced Battn HqQrs, which was situated with the M.G. Reserve attached to 2/R.W.F. The 115th Inf. Bde were forced back on to the outskirts of MORVAL on a line facing N.E. 9th S.W.B. Range remained with 25 men in a post 500 yds in front of this line. 2 Coys of the 10th D.W.R. were pushed out to form a defensive left flank. This operation was successful & prisoners were taken by them. Touch was established by	49.N. 6 sheet

115/38

Vol 50

2nd BATTALION
ROYAL WELSH
FUSILIERS

WAR DIARY or INTELLIGENCE SUMMARY

Army Form C. 2118.

Place	Date	Hour	Summary of Events and Information	Remarks and references to Appendices
SAILLY SAILLESEL	2.9.18		The left Coy of these two flank defence Coys with the 17th Div. about 800 yds S. of LE TRANSLOY. A gap of about 700 yds existed between the left of the 2/7 R.W.Fus and the right of the defensive left flank Coys. This was filled by a post thrown out from Battn. H.Qrs. at 6.0 p.m. The 113th Inf. Bde attacked SAILLY SAILLESEL from MORVAL. This attack gained the main road running through the N. of SAILLY SAILLESEL. Enabled the 115th Inf. Bde to form on the light Railway immediately to the W. of SAILLY SAILLESEL. Regiments in the Bde formed as follows in view of carrying out the attack the following day :— 2/RWF (organised in 2 Coys) on the right. 10th Welch on the left. 17th RWF in support (on the MORVAL-ROCQUIGNY Broad Guage Railway). The M.G. section of C. Coy. M.G.C. attacked to 2/R.W.F. remained in front of LE TRANSLOY guarding the left flank with troops of 10th A.W.R still forming a defensive left flank. At 5.0 p.m. the 115th Inf. Bde was to attack LES MESNIL-EN-ARROUAISE and secure the Brunch line to a point 1200 yds. S. of this village. Orders of battle, 115th Inf. Bde. 7th R.O.F.us (organised in 2 Coys) on the right. 10th Welch on the left. 17th RWF in support a Battalion of the 113th Inf. Bde was to be formed up on the left flank of the attack. The troops were to make good LOON COPSE on the EASTERN outskirts of SAILLY SAILLESEL ready to move forward at 5.0 p.m. The enemy however were found to be still in the village although it had been reported clear. The troops had therefore to fight their way through SAILLY SAILLESEL. This was carried on throughout the night Sept. 2/3rd. and the 2/R.W.F. reached a point 500yds. beyond the village. The Battn. of the 113th Bde. which was to operate on the left of the 115 Inf. Bde was similarly held up. During the night the enemy made an attack against the left flank of the 113th Bde 2 Coys of the 14th Inf. Bde. which was in support were thrown out on this flank as a defensive left flank. At Dawn of Sept 3rd the enemy were found to have withdrawn.	

Army Form C. 2118.

WAR DIARY
or
INTELLIGENCE SUMMARY.
(Erase heading not required.)

Place	Date	Hour	Summary of Events and Information	Remarks and references to Appendices
LES. MESNIL	3.9.18.		The 38th Division continued its advance. The 113th Inf. Bde. was to occupy LES MESNIL in ARROUASE and the trench system just EAST of it. The 115th Inf. Bde. was to occupy the trench system from the right of the 113th Inf. Bde. into ST MARTINS WOOD where the Brigade was to join up with the 18th Division. The 114th Inf. Bde. was on the completion of the above operation, to pass through & force the TORTILLE RIVER, and gain the heights overlooking it. The 115th Inf. Bde. was disposed as follows. 17 R. Btn. on the right, 10 Welsh on the left, 2nd R.W.F. in support.	
	4.9.18.		Batn. in same position. 3 Reinforcement Officers joined. YES EABORN, GRIFFITH - PARKINSON. Battalion formed into 1 Coy of 4 platoons - strength about 90 ORR.	
	5.9.18.		Battalion relieved by 21st Division. 15th D.L.I. taking over Brigade area. The Battalion moved back to huts & bivouacs S. of LES. BOUEFS. Very wet evening.	
S. of LES BOUEFS	6.9.18.		Bt. Lt. Col. C.C. NORMAN, DSO. assumed command of Battalion. Baths for men. General cleaning up, reorganisation and refitting.	

WAR DIARY
or
INTELLIGENCE SUMMARY.
(Erase heading not required.)

Army Form C-2118.

Place	Date	Hour	Summary of Events and Information	Remarks and references to Appendices
S. of LES BOEUFS	7.9.18		Battalion in same place Refitting and reorganising	
"	8.9.18		Church services, morning. L. Gun practice on range.	
"	9.9.18		Refitting. L. Gun. Lewis Gun practice. Concert given by W.W.G. Party.	
E. of LECHELLE	10.9.18		Battalion and transport moved in the afternoon to E. of LECHELLE. Wet day.	
"	11.9.18		Officers reconnoitred this held by 50th Bde near GOUZEAUCOURT. Battalion moved forward and relieved 9th E. YORKS in this sector. Good relief. A Coy front. B Left front sup. C Support. D Support.	
GOUZEAUCOURT	12.9.18		Gas shelling near Bn. HQrs.	
	13.9.18		2nd Lieut heavily shelled. 2nd Lt T. PARKINSON killed. about 20 Casualties. Enemy attacked our front at 9.20am after heavy barrage on our front, support lines. Beaten off by L. Guns + Rifle fire. A few enemy penetrated into trench on left and were driven out by L. Gun leaving 5 killed in the trench & others died were found later in front of our of our posts. Mass of attack on B Coy front and driven off by them. Low flying EA tried by L.G. fire. B Coy. and seen to descend. Gas enjoined later by R.A.F. Int. Company relief D relieving B + C relieving A.	
	14.9.18		Quiet day. Gas shelling of area around Battn. HQrs. 3 Casualties.	
	15.9.18		Quiet day.	
	16.9.18		Fairly Quiet day. Battn. relieved by 10th LANCS. FUS. night of 16/17. Slow relief.	
N. of EQUANCOURT	17.9.18		Battalion marched to area around another road N. of EQUANCOURT. Baths for Battalion 8-11.0am. Cleaning up + refitting	

WAR DIARY
or
INTELLIGENCE SUMMARY.

(Erase heading not required.)

Army Form C. 2118.

Instructions regarding War Diaries and Intelligence Summaries are contained in F. S. Regs., Part II. and the Staff Manual respectively. Title pages will be prepared in manuscript.

Place	Date	Hour	Summary of Events and Information	Remarks and references to Appendices
	17.9.18		The following awarded MM by Corps Commander. E Corps. 6982. Cpl J. Ens. "A" Coy. 5275. L/C J. Dean. "C" Coy. 9439. Sgt J. Varcoe. "CH. "C" Coy. 6073. Pte O.H. Owen. "D" Coy. 5561.7. L/Cpl T. Fidler. "D" Coy. 9364. L/Cpl G. Lee. "A" Coy.	
FINS RIDGE	18.9.18		Battn. relieved by 2nd A.S.H. & moved forward at 6.15am to trenches at FINS RIDGE. Brigade in reserve during attack by 3rd & 4th Armies. Moved at 5.0pm to trenches N.E. of DESSART WOOD.	
DESSART WOOD	19.9.18		Brigade relieved 113th & 114th Bde. in line W. of GOUZEAUCOURT. Battalion relieved 2 Coys of 13th & 1 Coy 16th R.S.F. wo. Good relief. Battn. H.Q. in GOUZEAUCOURT. Battn. H.Qrs. together with 9th K.O.S.B. & 10th R.S. in S.E. corner of GOUZEAUCOURT WOOD. B Right Front, A Centre, C Left, D Left in support. Line subject to intermittent shelling and TMs.	
GOUZEAUCOURT	20.9.18		Fairly quiet day – intermittent shelling. Heavy barrage on front & support 7-8pm. Battalion relieved by 12th Manchester Regt. Slow relief that made finished halfway out. Battn. quartered in huts in LECHELLE'S	
N of BEAULENCOURT	22.9.18		Battalion with Transport moved by route march to camp of N of BEAULENCOURT. The following awarded MM by Corps Commander. 18315. L/Cpl W.M. Williams. 55624. Pte J.R. Williams. 8356. R/c G.Lee.	
	22.9.18		Baths and refitting	
	23.9.18		Refitting and reorganising. L Gun firing in range.	
	24.9.18		L Gun firing all Coys on range. Classes for B Scouts & bombing men under M.O.	
	25.9.18		As for 24th. Following reinforcement Officers joined Battn. for duty & posted to Coys as under: Lt. A.C.F. Griffith "A" 2/Lt C. Haslam "A" 2/Lt J.W. Mawley "B" 2/Lt R.H.L. Morgan "B" 2/Lt I. Thomas " D. Llewellyn "C" W. Wake " F. Kirk "D" S. Lloyd "D"	

Army Form C. 2118.

WAR DIARY
or
INTELLIGENCE SUMMARY.
(Erase heading not required.)

Instructions regarding War Diaries and Intelligence Summaries are contained in F. S. Regs., Part II. and the Staff Manual respectively. Title pages will be prepared in manuscript.

Place	Date	Hour	Summary of Events and Information	Remarks and references to Appendices
	26.9.18		Parade as for 25th. Awards by Corps Commander:- BAR to M.M. 7946 L/Cpl H. LEA, M.M.- 29695 Sjt. Tom JONES. 11255 Pte W. OLIVER.	
	27.9.18		Morning parade. Lunch to lunch practice attack. Classes in afternoon. Officers in company work under Second in command. N.C.O's in map reading under Major ADAMSON	
SOREL LE GRAND	28.9.18		Battalion moved by bus to SOREL-LE-GRAND and Co.'s huts & tents.	
"	29.9.18		Reconnoitring of forward area. Batt.n at 1 hr. notice to move.	
"	30.9.18		Batt.n still in SOREL-LE-GRAND. Lewis Gun instruction, training, R. Grenade throwing instruction in Camp.	

A. Ommanney Lieut. Col.
Comdg. 2nd Bn. Rif. Bde.

2 RWF Vol 51

50.11

WAR DIARY or INTELLIGENCE SUMMARY.

Army Form C. 2118.

Place	Date	Hour	Summary of Events and Information	Remarks and references to Appendices
SOREL-LE-GRAND.	1.10.18		Orders received informing us of Brigade to Officers.	
"	2.10.18		Rugby match against 10th S.W.Bs. in afternoon.	
"	3.10.18		Only to move. Battn. moved to trenches just out of LEMPIRE.	
LEMPIRE	4.10.18		Battn. moved to PIENNE to BONY - spuds from 9 a.m. to 3.45 p.m. midway between LEMPIRE & BONY. at 3.45 p.m. moved up to HINDENBURG supports E of BONY.	
E. of BONY	5.10.18		Knii in HINDENBURG line. Battn. left at 2.45 a.m. for LE CATELET. Battn. in LE CATELET thro' W. outskirts of village. H'Qrs. in cellar at X roads.	
LE CATELET	6.10.18		Moved from LE CATELET at 8.30 a.m. to bivd S 22. B 9.d. S. of BASKET WOOD. H'Qrs. in dug out S.E. cnr W. of PIENNE.	
W. of PIENNE.	7.10.18		Still as above. Orders received to co-operate in attack on VILLERS OUTREAUX. 10th S.W.B. on right, 17th R.W.F. on left. 2nd R.W.F. to mop up VILLERS OUTREAUX. 2nd R.W.F. to attack 1 Coy to follow up in rear of 17th R.W.F. & hold BEAUREVOIR LINE. Battn. in advance of 17th R.W.F.	
VILLERS OUTREAUX	8.10.18		Attack of 10th S.W.B. & 17th R.W.F. held up, but VILLERS OUTREAUX was taken later in the day by "B" Coy of 2nd R.W.F., working round to E. of village, + "A" Coy 2nd R.W.F. working round to the W. All too co-operated with tanks to mop up village. 2nd Lieut. A.C.F. GRIFFITH + 2nd Lieut W.E. JONES (Hon-ton) were killed & Capt. W.W. KIRKBY, 2nd Lieut. J.E. NICKSON & 2nd Lieut. J. MARLAND were wounded. Battn. spent the night at VILLERS OUTREAUX and the 33rd Division passed through us.	
"	9.10.18		2nd Lieut. EVANS-JONES, 2nd Lieut. R.H.H. MORGAN, C. HASLAM + J. BUTLER. reinforced. 113th & 114th Bde. moved to CLARY.	

Army Form C. 2118.

WAR DIARY
or
INTELLIGENCE SUMMARY.
(Erase heading not required.)

Instructions regarding War Diaries and Intelligence Summaries are contained in F. S. Regs., Part II. and the Staff Manual respectively. Title pages will be prepared in manuscript.

Place	Date	Hour	Summary of Events and Information	Remarks and references to Appendices
BERTRY.	10.10.18		The Battn. moved by march route to BERTRY at 15.00 Hours, 2/Lt. G. BOOTH being previously sent to billet the Battn. A draft of 112 O.Rs arrived at VILLERS OUTREAUX & were marched on to BERTRY.	
"	11.10.18		Battn. still in billets at BERTRY. All troops of the 115th Bde. spent a day of rest.	
TROISVILLE	12.10.18		The Battn. moved off at 12.30 Hours by march route to billets in TROISVILLE which had previously been arranged by 2/Lt. G. BOOTH. One Officer & one N.C.O. per Coy. & Bn. HQrs were sent up the line to reconnoitre & remained there the night & next day.	
"	13.10.18		The 115th Bde. relieved the 100th Bde. in the line on the SELLE RIVER. Battn. HQrs. situated at ROMBOURLIEUX FARM. "C" "D" Coys in front line & "A" "B" Coys in support.	
SELLE RIVER	14.10.18		Fairly quiet day, the Battn. HQrs was shelled intermittently.	
"	15.10.18		Gas projectors were fired and the H.A bombarded the Railway Embankment & Sunken Rd. E. of the RIVER.	
"	16.10.18		"A" "B" Coys relieved "C" "D" Coys at dusk. "D" Coy going into support "C" Coy into reserve on the LE. CATEAU. Rd.	
"	17.10.18		The 60th Div. attacked on our right & captured 1100 prisoners & LE. CATEAU. STN. 115th Bde. relieved by the 114th Bde. 2/R.W.F. relieved by 13/WELCH.Regt. Front Coys 2/R.W.F. by the 14/R.W.F. The Battn. then moved back to billets in TROISVILLE.	
TROISVILLE	18.10.18		Battn. were allotted to Battn.	

Army Form C. 2118.

WAR DIARY
or
INTELLIGENCE SUMMARY.
(Erase heading not required.)

Instructions regarding War Diaries and Intelligence Summaries are contained in F. S. Regs., Part II. and the Staff Manual respectively. Title pages will be prepared in manuscript.

Place	Date	Hour	Summary of Events and Information	Remarks and references to Appendices
TROISVILLE.	20.10.18		The Battn. moved at 05.00 Hours to support the 113th & 114th Bdes in an attack on AMERVAL RIDGE, the Bde being situated in Sunken Road W. of RIVER SELLE. R.W.F. behind ridge on ridge W. of the River. Battn returned to TROISVILLE about 18.00 Hours to billets previously occupied.	
"	21.10.18		The 115th Bde relieved the 114th Bde on the final objective of the 20th inst, 9 R.W.F. in Bde Reserve. "D" Coy being lent to 11/R.W.F. on left. "C" Coy to 10/S.W.B. on right. "A" & "B" Coys on the Railway E. of RIVER SELLE. Battn. H.Q. at RAMBOURLIEUX FARM (Mashup).	
RIVER SELLE.	22.10.18		A quiet day. The Battn relieved by units of 33rd Div. & returned to TROISVILLE.	
TROISVILLE.	23.10.18		The 115th Bde in support to 33rd Div in attack by V Corps in conjunction with Corps on right & left. The Battn moved from TROISVILLE at 05.00 Hrs to assembly positions on AMERVAL RIDGE. At mid-day Battn. moved to RICHEMONT & at dusk occupied areas objectives on the neighbourhood of CROIX & CALUYAUX. where the night was spent. B.H.Q. situated in CROIX.	
CROIX.	24.10.18		Battn. was called upon to fill possible gap between the 33rd & 18th Divisions. the Bde being in Reserve along the main FOREST-ENGLEFONTAINE ROAD.	
FOREST-ENGLEFONTAINE	25/26/10/18		Battn. unable to relieve the Welsh 33rd Bde, but relief was postponed 24 Hours until the 33rd Div. had completed capture of ENGLEFONTAINE. B.N. Bn moved to a more convenient place.	
"	26.10.18		The 115th Bde relieved 100th Bde in line. 7/10.2 relieving 1/WORCESTERS & 1/O.H.L.I. Relief started at 14.30 hrs. Completion of relief was delayed by also having to take over from 1/MIDDLESEX. The Bn. held right half of Div. front with line through Eastern & W. Halt of ENGLEFONTAINE. B.N. Coy at BRASSERIE.	

(A8604) Wt W1771/M2931 750,000 5/17 Sch. 52 Forms/C.2118/14

Army Form C. 2118.

WAR DIARY
or
INTELLIGENCE SUMMARY.
(Erase heading not required.)

Place	Date	Hour	Summary of Events and Information	Remarks and references to Appendices
BRASSERIE.	27.10.18		The Battn. was given a two fold role of consolidating any defensive line and acting as advanced guard to push back in line from main line of resistance the enemy outer Battn. on our right. Bn. at dawn, but failed. Bn. suffering several casualties from the enemy M.G. fire. A system of 'Piercing Contratack' was adopted & 'B' Coy attempted to capture two enemy posts about 300 yds from the front line. The attack was held up by heavy M.G. fire but as such the remaining Bn. advanced their line to 150 yds to 200 m.	
"	28.10.18		Bn. continued to push forward new line. 'C' Coy on the right. having a rough struggle in house to house on Route d'MCCA. otherwise a quiet day.	
"	29.10.18		Line advanced to 'C' Coy about 100 yds. The Battn. on our left raided enemy & were very successful. Foix ENGLEFONTAINE heavily shelled. The 115th Bde relieved by the 11th R.W.F. the 2/R.W.F. being relieved by 15/WELCH. On relief the Battn. returned to CALVYAUX, CROIX. Bttn. Hd.Qrs situated near CALVYAUX X ROADS.	
CROIX.	30.10.18		Battn. allotted to Battn. remainder of day allowed for 'cleaning up'. Weather fine.	
"	31.10.18		Bn. in same billets. — training & practice in close country fighting — wet day.	

D. Owen Capt & Adjt
for Major
Commdg. 2nd Battn. Royal Welch Fusiliers

SECRET.

Army Form C. 2118.

2 RWF
Vol 52

Jackson
51. N
5 sheets

WAR DIARY or INTELLIGENCE SUMMARY.

(Erase heading not required.)

Instructions regarding War Diaries and Intelligence Summaries are contained in F.S. Regs., Part II. and the Staff Manual respectively. Title pages will be prepared in manuscript.

Place	Date	Hour	Summary of Events and Information	Remarks and references to Appendices
CROIX.	1.11.18		Battalion in billets at CROIX. Attack practices in VENDEGIES WOOD — Fine day —	
ENGLEFONTAINE	2.11.18		115th Inf Bde relieved the 114th Bde in the line 2/R.W.F. on right. An H.Q. took over Support Coy. H.Q. in ENGLEFONTAINE. Relief complete at 5.30 p.m.	
	3.11.18		Quiet day — Preparations for attack.	
	4.11.18		The 38th Divn attacked the South Eastern outskirts of ENGLEFONTAINE and the FORÊT DE MORMAL. On the right the 18th Divn attacked & on the left the 17th Divn attacked. Zero was at 5.30 a.m. when the Divnl on the left was to open the attack. The 115 Bde was to open the attack of the 38th Divn at 3.40 + 45 attacked at 6.15 a.m. The order of battle of the 115th Inf Bde was, on the right 2/R.W.F. in the centre 10/S.W.B., on the left 17/R.W.F. Tank was allotted to each Battn. The Bn. was formed up by 5.30 a.m. The first objective the Brown Line, a Ride running roughly N & S. 500 yds East of the Western edge of the FORÊT DE MORMAL 'em the wood & first Brigade objective had been given which was the Western edge of the FORÊT DE MORMAL where Inf Bde would to capture the BLUE LINE were to trek thro' through the Left leaving the attack up to the Eastern Edge of the FORÊT DE MORMAL. The 18th Divn. attacked at 6.15 a.m. The mode of battle of the 115th Bde was as noted above and at 5 a.m. the Bn. was formed up to go over up the following order: Right front Coy "C" (Cpt) Left front Coy "D" Coy. Right support Coy "B" , Left support Coy "A" Coy. The tank allotted to the Bn. was not easy on the change of direction of trenches has to be carried out, & the tanks veered from 300 to 500 owing to the right	

WAR DIARY or INTELLIGENCE SUMMARY

Army Form C. 2118.

Place	Date	Hour	Summary of Events and Information	Remarks and references to Appendices
	4/11/18 cont		Nothing on a stream (RUISSEAU DES ECLUSETTES), which turns a great deal in its course. The front on the forming up line was about 500y + on the final objective about 1200y. The greater part of which was in a clearing. This meant that on reaching the Leap Frog line a third Tn had to push into the Front Line. The dispositions were ordered therefore, that on reaching the Leapfrog line B Ty would become the Right Front Tn, C Ty - the Centre Front Tn, A Ty leapfrogged through D Tn s became the Left Front Tn, D Tn remained in the Leapfrog line in Reserve. There were not sufficient troops within the Tn to completely mop up, + to have done so with troops of the Tn which became engaged in their houses, would have unduly delayed the advance, so B.Hrs was made responsible for the final mopping up of their houses. The Battn moved to the attack at 6.15am behind a very heavy and accurate barrage put up by the 38 Divl Artillery. The morning was very misty and though it made the keeping of direction difficult it hampered the enemy's movements considerably + was very helpful to the Battalion in moving operations, which was particularly heavy in M.G. + T.M. fire. The Tank allotted to the Bn. failed to appear, but one TANK MI, allotted to the 18th Bn., which had lost its way, was intercepted and rendered valuable service to the Regiment during the advance. During the whole advance there was a gap of about 400y between the Right of the Battalion and the Left of the Division on our Right and the enemy exploited the Gn. heavily with M.G. fire + T.M. fire from this flank. The Tank gave considerable help in keeping down this fire. By the final objective being occupied the Reserve (N° 4 D Tn) crossed the RUISSEAU DES ECLUSETTES (Ratum.	

WAR DIARY
or
INTELLIGENCE SUMMARY.
(Erase heading not required.)

Army Form C. 2118.

Instructions regarding War Diaries and Intelligence Summaries are contained in F. S. Regs., Part II. and the Staff Manual respectively. Title pages will be prepared in manuscript.

Place	Date	Hour	Summary of Events and Information	Remarks and references to Appendices
ENGLEFONTAINE	4.11.18 (cont)		Right Boundary) and cleared the enemy from just beyond the Right of the final Objective and the ground in rear as far back west as the village of HECQ. The Tpy dropped back during the manœuvre & formed a defensive Right flank to the Battn. A Coy A Coy in the meantime had moved into reserve in the position formerly occupied by D Coy, clearing an area on the ENGLEFONTAINE – HECQ Road where it crossed the RUSSEN & des ECLUSETTES. The Battn. captured: 1 Field Gun 6 Trench Mortars 28 Machine guns (light & heavy) The casualties were: 2/Lt WKC KEEPER, killed; 2/Lt G P JONESHM, C HASLAM, R E GRIFFITHS & Lt LLEWELLYN wounded. 10 O.R's killed, 65 O.R's wounded & missing. Enemy casualties: killed – about 40. Prisoners. 4 Officers, 120 O.R's approx. At 4.0 p.m. the Battn. returned to billets vacated in the morning. Battn. in same place - day spent in cleaning up & collecting captures.	
FORÊT-de-MORMAL	6.11.18		Battn. marched from billets to bivouacs in FORÊT de MORMAL. Day not perf?	
BERLAIMONT	7.11.18		Battn. marched to BERLAIMONT where it stayed for 4 hours afterwards proceeding to billets at AULNOYE.	
AULNOYE	8.11.18		The Battn. moved up to POT DE VIN at 3:30 am & took up position in field & returned to same billets at noon.	
	9.11.18		Day spent in cleaning up.	

Army Form C. 2118.

WAR DIARY
or
INTELLIGENCE SUMMARY.
(Erase heading not required.)

Instructions regarding War Diaries and Intelligence Summaries are contained in F. S. Regs., Part II. and the Staff Manual respectively. Title pages will be prepared in manuscript.

Place	Date	Hour	Summary of Events and Information	Remarks and references to Appendices
HULLUCH	10.11.18		115th Inf. Bde. practice Route March in the morning. Tire but cold.	
"	11.11.18		The Day spent in cleaning up and refitting. HOSTILITIES ceased at 11.00 HOURS. Parades under Coy arrangements. The G.O.C. addressed the Bde. (115) at 2.30pm.	
"	12.11.18		Baths allotted to the Battn. Baths uses formed.	
"	13.11.18		Parades under Coy arrangements — Cold —	
"	14.11.18		Brigade Route March. Capt. W.W. KIRKBY awarded the DSO & Lieut J.E. NICKSON a Bar to his MC & 2/Lt. H. Turner MM. the MC	
"	15.11.18		Later, in Coal Fatigue.	
"	16.11.18		Thanksgiving Service at 11.0am to Lieut HQ, R.A. & 115th Inf Br.	
"	17.11.18		Training under Company arrangements.	
"	18.11.18		Route March.	
"	19.11.18		Training under Company arrangements.	
"	20.11.18		Brigade Route March. Bath. Guest Night. D. Coy. R.S.M. & to Annual Bathe.	
"	21.11.18		Training under Company arrangements & bathe.	
"	22.11.18		Presentation of Medal Ribbons by the Bde. General at 11.00 hours. Recipients:-	
"	23.11.18		Lt.Col. J.B.COCKBURN (D.S.O), Major G.E.R. de MIREMONT, Capt. W.EVANS, 2/Lt. C.F.LARSON, 2/Lt. A. INCE & F.G. FERRIS the Military Cross. C.M.O. 13183 Y/Sgt G. EVANS (DCM + MM) D.C.M.— 20961 C/Sgt E. LEE, MM. 5894 CSM J BOWEN. 8233 C/Sgt T MEREDITH, 9045 A/RBMS J HUGHES M.M. + BAR — 1946 A/Sgt H. LEA & 6103 Pte O. OWENS, M.M.— 9126 C/Sgt E TROTMAN, 4341 Pte B.GARRIGAN 101102 Pte D. BENNION, 39695 Sgt W JONES, 200702 Cpl. W. PRICE, 15318 Pte N. WILLIAMS, 4936 Pte BROWN. M.S.M.— 4690 A/Sgt Birch W.DYER. MM. 37090 Pte W.M. HUMPHREYS, 9268 Pte W. MOORE, 11336 A/Sgt T FISHER	

Army Form C. 2118.

WAR DIARY
or
INTELLIGENCE SUMMARY.
(Erase heading not required.)

Instructions regarding War Diaries and Intelligence Summaries are contained in F. S. Regs., Part II. and the Staff Manual respectively. Title pages will be prepared in manuscript.

Place	Date	Hour	Summary of Events and Information	Remarks and references to Appendices
AUNOYE.	24.11.18		Church Services, Holy Communion Voluntary.	
"	25.11.18		Brigade Route March.	
"	26.11.18		Training under Company arrangements. Medical inspection for miners.	
"	27.11.18		Training under Company arrangements. Brigade Educational Classes - Boxing.	
"	28.11.18		" " " Company Boxing in afternoon.	
"	29.11.18		Brigade Route March.	
"	30.11.18		Battalion Route March. - Inspection of billets by Commanding Officer.	

M. Atkinson
Major.
Comdg 2nd Battn. Royal Welch Fusiliers

2 RW

WAR DIARY
or
INTELLIGENCE SUMMARY.
(Erase heading not required.)

Army Form C. 2118.

Place	Date	Hour	Summary of Events and Information	Remarks and references to Appendices
AULNOYE	1/12/18		Church Parade.	
"	2/12/18		Lt. D. Roberts Morgan D.C.M, M.M. joined from 13th Bn. R.W.Fus. Sgt. Moskins & L/Sgt. Jacques awarded Military Medal. Training as per Training Programme.	
"	3/12/18		Lecture by Adjutant on Extension of Service. H.M. The King passed through AULNOYE & inspected Battalion.	
"	4/12/18		Colour Party consisting of Lt. C.S. Roberts, 2/Lt. A.L. Jones, Lot/Sgt G. Bracken, Sgt E. Croman, M.M. Sgt. F. Horley, M.M & W/Cpl R. Williams proceeded to WREXHAM, U.K., to get Battalion Colours. Brigade Route March cancelled.	
"	5/12/18		Brigade route march. Capt. F. Holden (C. Coy) Lt. J.P. Jones (B. Coy) Lt Eames (D. Coy) 2/Lt. E. Giles (A. Coy) joined Battalion.	
"	6/12/18		Training as per Training Programme. Battalion bathed.	
"	7/12/18		Battalion Drill 9-30 to 10-30. Interior economy.	
"	8/12/18		Church Parade.	
"	9/12/18		Training as per Training Programme.	
"	10/12/18		Inspection of Companies in various duties by Brigade Commander.	
"	11/12/18		Battalion Route March cancelled. Weather bad.	
"	12/12/18		Training as per Training Programme. Following decorations awarded:—	

D.S.O. Major G.E.R. de Miremont, M.C.
M.C. A/Capt. E. Howell Evans A/Capt. J. Butler, D.C.M.
       2/Lt. A.L. Jones, 2/Lt. F. Kirk, C.S.M. J. Baldwin, M.M.
BAR TO D.C.M. C.S.M. J.E. Bowen, D.C.M.
D.C.M. Sgt. M. Luter. L/Cpl. H. Thorndyke.

WAR DIARY
or
INTELLIGENCE SUMMARY.
(Erase heading not required.)

Army Form C. 2118.

Place	Date	Hour	Summary of Events and Information	Remarks and references to Appendices
AULNOYE	12-12-18		Court of Enquiry:- President, CAPT. F. HOLDEN. Members, 2/LT. J.H. MORGAN. 2/LT. W.E. LEPPARD. to enquire into illegal absence of PTE. W. MEAD. "D" Coy.	
"	13-12-18		Battalion route march. Roads bad.	
"	14-12-18		Battalion Drill & Interior economy.	
"	15-12-18		Church Parade.	
"	16-12-18		Training as per Training Programme.	
"	17-12-18		do	
"	18-12-18		do	
"	19-12-18		do	
"	20-12-18		do & baths for Battalion.	
"	21-12-18		Brigade route march. - Railway bridge - PETIT MAUBEUGE - LEVAL - MONCEAU ST. VAAST.	
"	22-12-18		G.O.C. inspected Transport.	
"	23-12-18		Church Parade.	
"	24-12-18		Brigade route march. Heavy rain. Roads very bad.	
"	24-12-18		Training as per Training Programme.	
"	25-12-18		Xmas Day. MAJOR W.G.E.R. de MIREMONT. D.S.O. M.C. President, and LT. C.J. ROBERTS, Member, of F.G.C.M. Church Parade.	
"			Men's Dinner 2-30 p.m. Concert in Recreation Hut at 5 p.m.	
"	26-12-18		Company Drill from 10-00 to 11-30 hrs. Games & football in the afternoon.	
"	27-12-18		Brigade route march. Battalion headed column. Route:- POT DE VIN & PETIT MAUBEUGE.	
"	28-12-18		Training as per Training Programme.	

WAR DIARY or INTELLIGENCE SUMMARY.

Army Form C. 2118.

Place	Date	Hour	Summary of Events and Information	Remarks and references to Appendices
AULNOYE	29.12.18		Battalion commenced march to QUERRIEU area. 1st stage through Forest of MORMAL to ENGLEFONTAINE and HECQ. Weather very wet & stormy. Battalion billeted for night 29/30th in HECQ. Lt C.J. ROBERTS was in charge of advance billeting party. Transport moved independently under Lt P.F. KUNKLER. Taking 5 days to reach new area, staying for the night at NEUVILLY.	
HECQ.	30/12/18		Moved returned from HECQ to INCHY in better weather. Route – through ENGLEFONTAINE – CROIX FOREST – NEUVILLY. Battalion billeted for night in INCHY. Lt C.J. ROBERTS did billeting.	
INCHY.	31.12.18		Third & last day of move. Battalion embussed at 07.30 on main INCHY – CAMBRAI Rd, & proceeded across the battle devastated area via CAMBRAI – BAPAUME & ALBERT reaching the new camp, near BLANGY TRONVILLE about 15.30 hrs. The camp is pleasantly situated, but still requires a great deal of work to complete it.	

W.R. A. Richmond.
Major.
Commdg. 2nd Bn. Royal Welch Fusiliers.

WAR DIARY or INTELLIGENCE SUMMARY

Army Form C. 2118.

2 RWF

Place	Date	Hour	Summary of Events and Information	Remarks and references to Appendices
Blangy Tronville	1/1/19	—	New Year's Day. Battalion in Camp at Blangy Tronville. Companies were at the disposal of Company Commanders for cleaning up and fatigues.	
"	2/1/19	—	Battalion on Wood Fatigue in Camp under Major Adamson.	
"	3/1/19	—	2/Lt W. Hawley left Battalion for a course.	
"	4/1/19	—	Companies were at the disposal of Coy Commanders and outfatigues. Court of Inquiry held to enquire into the loss of Government rifles. President Capt S.E.B. Barkworth, members Lieut I.Thomas, G. Jones.	
	5/1/19		Church parade Service C.of.E. 2nd and 7th Bns. R.W.F. involved. Room at Blangy Tronville.	
	6/1/19		Battalion on work under Major Adamson.	
	7/1/19		A.C. and D. Coys were training B Coy on work under Major Adamson.	
	8/1/19		Brigade route march. Route East of Glissy S.E. of Longeau N. of St. Nicolas Blangy Tronville.	
	9/1/19		A and B Coys on work. Capt Barkworth left at 1030 hrs for SAILLY LAURETTE to round up Australian Deserters. 2 captured on arr...	

53. N.
4 sheet

WAR DIARY or INTELLIGENCE SUMMARY

Army Form C. 2118.

Place	Date	Hour	Summary of Events and Information	Remarks and references to Appendices
Blangy-Tronville	10/1/19	—	Island W of SAILLY LAURETTE and brought back to camp under escort	
	11/1/19		Coys returned at 15.30 hours, remainder of the Battalion were on fatigue. C and D Companies were working on Horse Standings etc under Major Adamson. A and B Coys Bathed.	
	12/1/19		C.O's inspection; all Coys paraded full marching order. Coys at the disposal of Major R.A. Adamson for the remainder of the day.	
	13/1/19		Church Parade C of E in 17th R.W.F. recreation hut	
	14/1/19		Battalion at the disposal of Major R.A. Adamson	
	15/1/19		Battalion at the disposal of Major R.A. Adamson	
			Battalion route march - route South of Blangy Tronville Battalion Cadey Bois L' Abbé Blangy.	
	16/1/19		Battalion on practice parade for G.O.C's inspection	
	17/1/19		Battalion at the disposal of Major Adamson for Camp fatigues and improvements	
			G.O.C's inspection cancelled owing to illness of the General.	
	18/1/19		Battalion on Tactical scheme under C.O. Capt E. Howell Evans left on course	
	19/1/19		Church parade in 17th R.W.F. recreation hut	

Army Form C. 2118.

WAR DIARY
or
INTELLIGENCE SUMMARY.
(Erase heading not required.)

Instructions regarding War Diaries and Intelligence Summaries are contained in F. S. Regs., Part II. and the Staff Manual respectively. Title pages will be prepared in manuscript.

Place	Date	Hour	Summary of Events and Information	Remarks and references to Appendices
Blangy-Tronville	20/1/19		G.O.C's inspection. Battalion paraded in full marching order afterwards all huts and institutions in Camp.	
	21/1/19		Companies were at the disposal of Major Adamson for work & improvements in the Camp.	
	22/1/19		Battalion bathed & worked under Major Adamson	
	23/1/19		Battalion on Camp improvements under Major Adamson. Brigade field officer of the day instituted	
	24/1/19		Battalion route march, route: Blangy. N of St. Nicolas. E of Longpre. An back to Camp	
	25/1/19		Companies on Camp improvements under Major Adamson 9777 Sergt. G. Bracken awarded M.S.M	
	26/1/19		Church parade in 17th R.W.F. recreation hut.	
	27/1/19		Companies were at the disposal of Major R.A. Adamson, on improvements in Camp.	
	28/1/19		Companies were at the disposal of Major R.A. Adamson on improvements in Camp	

WAR DIARY
or
INTELLIGENCE SUMMARY.
(Erase heading not required.)

Army Form C. 2118.

Place	Date	Hour	Summary of Events and Information	Remarks and references to Appendices
Blangy Tronville	29/1/19		Companies were at the disposal of Major R.A. Adamson on improvements in camp. Boxing Tournament at 11-30 by 2nd R. W.F. represented the 115 Infantry Brigade. Represented 113th R. W.F. represented the 113th Infantry Brigade.	
	30/1/19		Companies were at the disposal of Major R.A. Adamson for work on Camp. Returned to despatches by Lt. Col. C.C. Norman D.S.O. & Lieut. D.S.O. Sergt. W. Evans D.C.M. M.M. Capt. W. Kirkby D.S.O.	
	31/1/19		Coys at the disposal of Major R.A. Adamson for work in Camp improvements. No 8107 Sergt F. Hanley M.M. awarded D.C.M. No 9826 Sergt E.C. Loram M.M. awarded D.C.M. & Meritorious Service List. Demobilisation up to and ending 31st Jan/1919 the numbers demobilised from the Battalion are	

OFFICERS 0
OTHER RANKS
France 206
Otr. Occupation 159
Total 365

R. Evans Capt
for Major
Cmdg 17th Welsh Rgt

WAR DIARY
or
INTELLIGENCE SUMMARY.
(Erase heading not required.)

Army Form C. 2148.

2 RWF Vol 54

5H.N.
2 vmts

Place	Date	Hour	Summary of Events and Information	Remarks and references to Appendices
Beauget Gonville	1/2/19	-	Battalion engaged in Camp improvements & fatigues. Divine service in YMCA Hut 17.10.30 by Camp "My experience as a prisoner of war in Germany" by Rev Basil O'Meehan.	
"	2/2/19	-	Church Parade service C of E 10.15hrs RC on parade at 09.30hrs. R.Catholic 09.30hrs.	
"	3/2/19	-	Camp improvements & fatigues. No of men sent by Lorries Sgt A Coy Batt Concert in the Recreation Hut on the occasion of its opening.	
	4/2/19	-	Baths at GUIGY for the Battn 103 hrs 1616 other ranks. Transfer of B Coy Lewis Guns.	
	5/2/19	-	Camp improvements & fatigues Capt. T. BUTLER, M.C. DCM went in charge of Batn party conveying troops for demobilisation "Education Leave" to R.W.F. Depot that on "Optimates in Egypt."	
	6/2/19	-	Camp improvements & fatigues. Hut 1030 hrs 2/Lt R.Cot PERKINS DSO 18th Welsh Regt in survival.	
	7/2/19	-	Camp improvements & fatigues. H.R.H. the Prince of Wales, maria the Batt accompanied by B.O.C.Gner H.A.H. inspected the Camp while the men were all in their quarters and afterwards invited officers to left at 14.00 hrs	
	8/2/19	-	Camp improvements & fatigues.	
	9/2/19	-	Church Parade services of Longuea Labour by 1/19 RS GWH BOURNS. MC Curry 151 F Coy RE on purpose of	
	10/2/19	-	Camp improvements & fatigues labour by 1/19 RS GWH BOURNS. MC Curry 151 F Coy RE on purpose of service of the Divisional Sanitary Board.	
	11/2/19	-	Camp improvements & fatigues.	
	12/2/19	-	Camp improvements & fatigues.	
	13/2/19	-	Camp improvements Batn Route march to QUAREVIEU to view presentation shield to H.R.H the Prince of Wales by the 21st RWF (Army of Occupation) Baths at GUSY.	
	14/2/19	-	Camp improvement.	
	15/2/19	-	Church Parade service C of E left the Batn for duty with the 21st RWF (Army of Occupation)	
	16/2/19	-	Camp improvement & fatigues. The Regimental Band reinforcements joined the Bn from the Depot WREXHAM	
	17/2/19	-	Camp improvement & fatigues 53. Q.R. under Band master CLANCY	

Army Form C. 2118.

WAR DIARY
or
INTELLIGENCE SUMMARY.
(Erase heading not required.)

2nd BATTALION ROYAL WELCH FUSILIERS.
No .... Date ....

Instructions regarding War Diaries and Intelligence Summaries are contained in F. S. Regs., Part II. and the Staff Manual respectively. Title pages will be prepared in manuscript.

Place	Date	Hour	Summary of Events and Information	Remarks and references to Appendices
BLANGY TRONVILLE	18/2/19	–	Camp improvement & Fatigues	
"	19/2/19	–	Camp improvement & Fatigues	
	20/2/19	–	Camp improvement & Fatigues	
	21/2/19	–	Battn. Route march og.3ohrs. to BOVES. accompanied by the Band. 17 R.W.F. joined the Bn. for this march.	
	22/2/19	–	Camp improvement & Fatigues. Battn. at GUISY for Band & Drums.	
	23/2/19	–	Church Parade Service	
	24/2/19	–	Camp improvement & Fatigues	
	25/2/19	–	Butts at GUISY 08.00 to 10.00hrs	
	26/2/19	–	Camp improvement & Fatigues	
	27/2/19	–	Camp improvement & Fatigues. Band & Drums visited Battle Area in motor lorries & shown scenes of interest by the Adjutant	
	28/2/19	–	Camp improvement & Fatigues.	

During month of February the number demobilised from the Battn. are as under

Officers 0R.
—————————
    8   202.

Total number demobilised to date.

Officers OR.
—————————
   3   581.
  ≡4

1/3/19

W Sam Capt
for Major
Comdg 2nd R.W.F.

WAR DIARY
or
INTELLIGENCE SUMMARY.
(Erase heading not required.)

Army Form C. 2118.

2 RWF
Vol 5-5

Place	Date	Hour	Summary of Events and Information	Remarks and references to Appendices
Scrum H	1.3.19		1st South Bn. Command Regimental Dinner in Canbrai attended by Officers 17 RWF. The guests included Maj Gen T.B. Chaplin C.M.G. D.S.O. Brig Gen H. J. Evans C.B. M.G. Lt.Col. C.C. Norman D.S.O. and Lt.Col. Howes D.S.O. Late our Brigadier. 16 Officers attending to Dinner.	
	2.3.19		Sunday. Paul. Came into Area at 23.00 hrs today. Church Parade Service. Band Program. D.Camp 13.00 - 14.45 hrs. 115 Bde Hdrs. G.C.S.y 16.00 - 17.00 hrs.	
	3.3.19		Camp Fatigue.	
	4.3.19		Camp Fatigue.	
	5.3.19		Battn. Pay [Rest] 10.00 , 11.00 hrs.	
	6.3.19		Camp Fatigue	
	7.3.19		Camp Fatigue. Band played at Brit. A. Canteen	
	8.3.19		Camp Fatigue. Pay. Band played at 113 Bde. Westny and Cantry.	
	9.3.19		Church Parade Service. Band held to continue to Smoke engagement at Hautn	
	10.3.19		Camp Fatigue.	
	11.3.19		Camp Fatigue. Summary of Evidence taken in case of F.G.C.M.	
	12.3.19		Camp Fatigue	
	13.3.19		Camp Fatigue.	
	14.3.19		Camp Fatigue.	
	15.3.19		Batn. Fety 10.00 - 11.30 hrs. F.G.C.M. on Pte. Scanes held in Camp 10.00 hrs. Parade Wire 10.30. 113 Bde Hd. C.O.'s call 3.30. Am.	
	16.3.19		Church Parade Service.	
	17.3.19		Camp Fatigue. 113th Bde. move into the camp.	
	18.3.19		Camp Fatigue.	
	19.3.19		Camp Fatigue.	
	20.3.19		Camp Fatigue.	

55 V.

WAR DIARY
or
INTELLIGENCE SUMMARY

Army Form C. 2118.

Place	Date	Hour	Summary of Events and Information	Remarks and references to Appendices
Clary Ty Noeux les	21.3.19		Camp Dangier	
	22.3.19		Lecture Read by O.C. & Camp Commandant and clothing issue was on Camp. Party. "C" "D" R.W.F. and No 3 W.B.? moved into the Camp. Douses [?] beds opened Hospital.	
	23.3.19		Church Parade Services	
	24.3.19		Camp Recreation. D.G.C.M. on Bosses. Roll in Camp 10-30 hr.	
	25.3.19		Camp Fatigues	
	26.3.19		Camp Fatigues	
	27.3.19		Camp Fatigues	
	28.3.19		Camp Fatigues. Games in Recreation Hut 6pm	
	29.3.19		Camp Fatigues. Pay.	
	30.3.19		Church Parade Services	
	31.3.19		Camp Fatigues	

During the month the following have been admitted to Hospital:

	Officers	O/Ranks
	1	26
		5
		8

Total admitted to Hospital from the Battalion
up to 31-3-19

No 26th Bn. R.W. Fus.

2 o.r. Nurses
40 8 Other occupation
61 4 Total

R. Atkinson
Lieut. Col.
Comdg. 26th Bn. R.W. Fus.

Army Form C. 2118.

2nd BATTALION ROYAL WELCH FUSILIERS.

No. .... Date 1/5/19

WAR DIARY
or
INTELLIGENCE SUMMARY.
(Erase heading not required)

Instructions regarding War Diaries and Intelligence Summaries are contained in F. S. Regs., Part II. and the Staff Manual respectively. Title pages will be prepared in manuscript.

Place	Date	Hour	Summary of Events and Information	Remarks and references to Appendices
Blangy Tronville	1/4/19		Baths for the Battalion at GLISY.	
	2/4/19		Camp Fatigues. Wood carrying.	
	3/4/19		" "	
	4/4/19		" " Rugby Football Match, 115th Bde v 113th Bde. 115th Bde won. Concert in 114th Bde.Rec.Hut.	
	5/4/19		Bath for Band at GLISY. Pay. Rugby Football Match. 115th Bde v 114th Bde. 115th Bde lost.	
	6/4/19		Church Parade Services with Band. Band played in Camp 12.00 to 12.45 hrs. and at GLISY 16.00 hrs.	
	7/4/19		Divisional Cadre Route March 10.00 hours.	
	8/4/19		Camp Fatigues. Association Football Match.	
	9/4/19		" " Concert in 114th Bde.Rec.Hut.	
	10/4/19		" " Pay.	
	11/4/19		" " Concert in 114th Bde.Rec.Hut.	
	12/4/19		Church Parade Services with Band. Band Programme as usual.	
	13/4/19		Divisional Route March.	
	14/4/19		Camp Fatigues.	
	15/4/19		" " Symphony Concert. Divisional Cadre Orchestra in 114th Bde.Rec.Hut.	
	16/4/19		" "	
	17/4/19		" " Fire in camp. Rec.hut accidentally burnt down. No one injured. Band at MONTIERES.	
	18/4/19		Regimental Court of Inquiry on Fire.	
	19/4/19		Camp Fatigues. Pay.	
	20/4/19		Easter Sunday. Church Parade Services with Band. Usual Sunday Band programme.	
	21/4/19		Camp Fatigues.	
	22/4/19		" "	
	23/4/19		" "	
	24/4/19		Band played at 5 Corps Con. Camp Sports, SAVEUSE in the afternoon and at MONTIERES in evening.	
	25/4/19		Band " A.I.F. Sports VILLERS BRETONNEAUX. Brig.Gen.H.deFree C.B.C.M.G., C.O. 115th Inf.Bde. left the Div. for England.	
	26/4/19		Church Parade Services. Band played at Anzac Memorial Service at VILLERS BRETONNEAUX.	
	27/4/19		Camp Fatigues. Pay. 1 Bandboy Killed and 3 wounded by a bomb on a dump near Camp. Wounded Boys dressed and evacuated to Hospital.	
	28/4/19		Military Funeral of Bandboy H. Williams. Buried in AUSTRAL CEMETERY (AMIENS-V. BRETT. road).	
	29/4/19		Bde.Court of Inquiry on Sat. accident. Lt.Col.G.E.R.deMIREMONT D.S.O., M.C. relinquished command of Battalion and left to join 48th.R.Fus (Russian Relief Force).	
	30/4/19		Camp Fatigues.	

www.ingramcontent.com/pod-product-compliance
Lightning Source LLC
Chambersburg PA
CBHW081246170426
43191CB00037B/2057